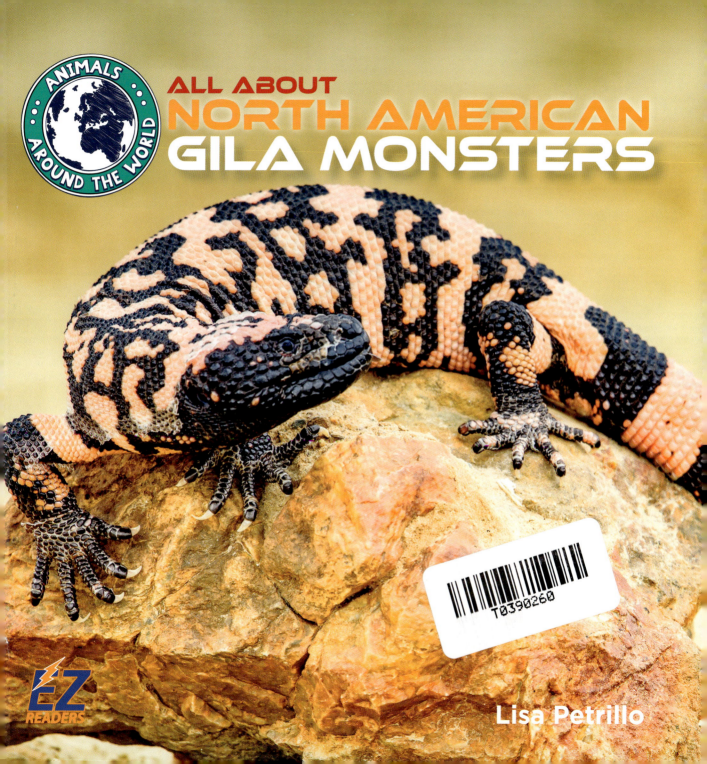
# ALL ABOUT NORTH AMERICAN GILA MONSTERS

Animals Around the World

Lisa Petrillo

EZ Readers

## Creating Young Nonfiction Readers

*EZ Readers* lets children delve into nonfiction at beginning reading levels. Young readers are introduced to new concepts, facts, ideas, and vocabulary.

## Tips for Reading Nonfiction with Beginning Readers

### Talk about Nonfiction
Begin by explaining that nonfiction books give us information that is true. The book will be organized around a specific topic or idea, and we may learn new facts through reading.

### Look at the Parts
Most nonfiction books have helpful features. Our *EZ Readers* include a Contents page, an index, and color photographs. Share the purpose of these features with your reader.

### Contents
Located at the front of a book, the Contents displays a list of the big ideas within the book and where to find them.

### Index
An index is an alphabetical list of topics and the page numbers where they are found.

### Glossary
Located at the back of the book, a glossary contains key words/phrases that are related to the topic.

### Photos/Charts
A lot of information can be found by "reading" the charts and photos found within nonfiction text. Help your reader learn more about the different ways information can be displayed.

With a little help and guidance about reading nonfiction, you can feel good about introducing a young reader to the world of *EZ Readers* nonfiction books.

---

**Mitchell Lane**
PUBLISHERS

2001 SW 31st Avenue
Hallandale, FL 33009
www.mitchelllanepub.com

Copyright © 2025 by Mitchell Lane Publishers. All rights reserved. No part of this book may be reproduced without written permission from the publisher. Printed and bound in the United States of America.

First Edition, 2025.

Author: Lisa Petrillo
Designer: Ed Morgan
Editor: Sharon F. Doorasamy

Names/credits:
Title: All About North American Gila Monsters / by Lisa Petrillo
Description: Hallandale, FL : Mitchell Lane Publishers, [2025]

Series: Animals Around the World
Library bound ISBN: 9781680204193
eBook ISBN: 9781680204209
Paperback ISBN: 9798892601368

EZ readers is an imprint of Mitchell Lane Publishers

Library of Congress Cataloging-in-Publication Data
Names: Petrillo, Lisa, author.
Title: All about North American gila monsters / by Lisa Petrillo.
Description: First edition. | Hallandale, FL : EZ Readers, an imprint of Mitchell Lane Publishers, 2020. | Series: Animals around the world-North American animals | Includes bibliographical references and index.
Identifiers: LCCN 2018030965| ISBN 9781680204193 (library bound) | ISBN 9781680204209 (ebook)
Subjects: LCSH: Gila monster—Juvenile literature.
Classification: LCC QL666.L247 P44 2020 | DDC 597.95/952—dc23
LC record available at https://lccn.loc.gov/2018030965

Photo credits: Freepik.com, Shutterstock.com, Getty Images, p. 6-7 Reptiles4all/Getty Images, p. 10-11 Kwiktor Getty Images, p. 12-13 Rick & Nora Bowers / Alamy Stock Photo, mapchart.net

# CONTENTS

| | |
|---|---|
| **Gila Monsters** | **4** |
| **Where Do Gila Monsters Live?** | **22** |
| **Interesting Facts** | **23** |
| **Parts of a Gila Monster** | **23** |
| **Glossary** | **24** |
| **Further Reading** | **24** |
| **On the Internet** | **24** |
| **Index** | **24** |

Gila monsters are lizards. They live in dry and rocky deserts.

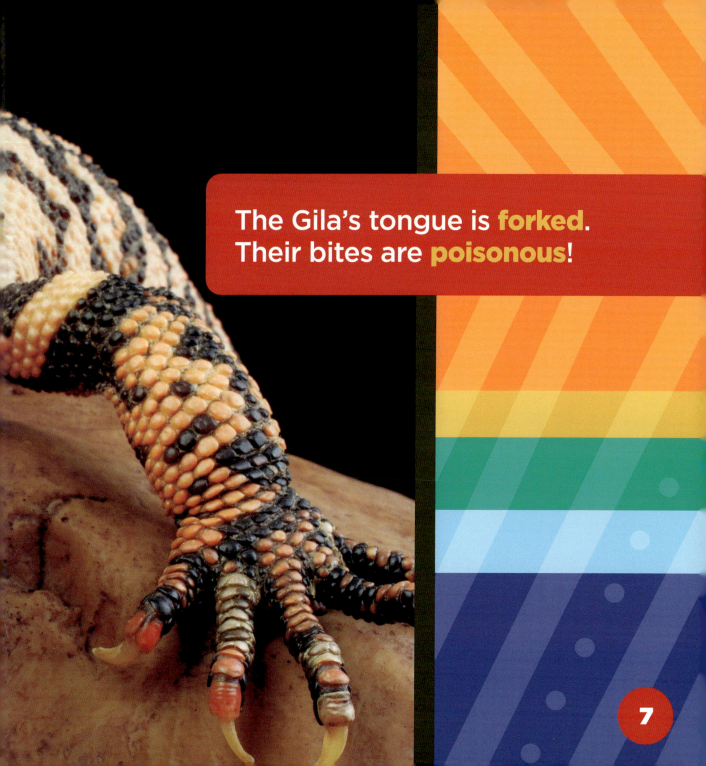

The Gila's tongue is **forked**. Their bites are **poisonous**!

Gila skin is made of **scales**. The scales protect them from enemies.

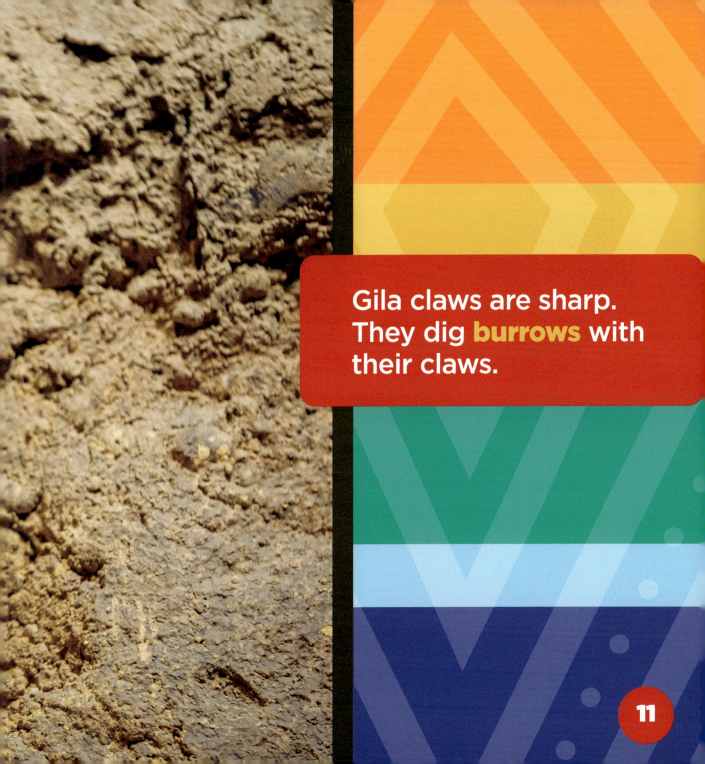

Gila claws are sharp. They dig **burrows** with their claws.

The Gila's claws help them hunt. They hunt frogs, rodents, and worms. The monster only eats a few times a year.

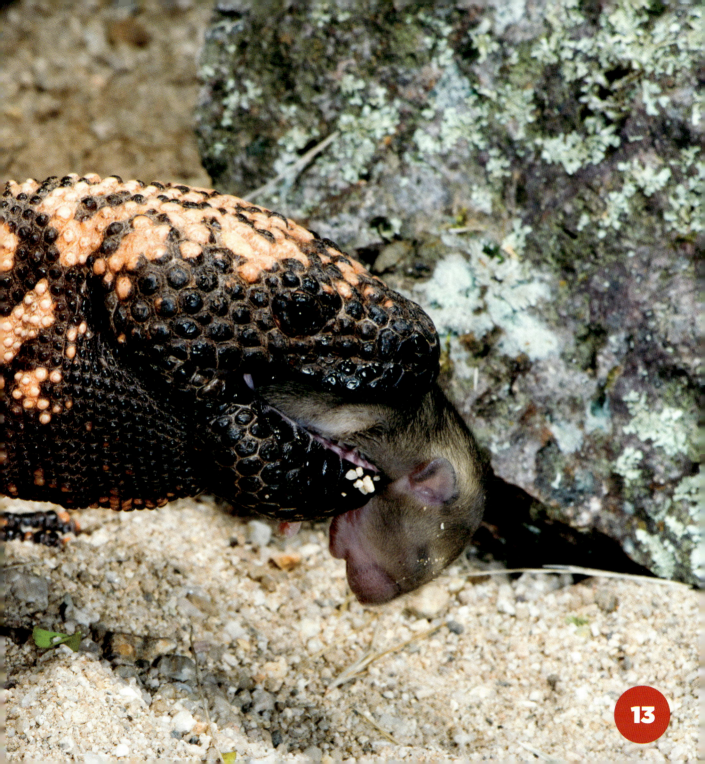

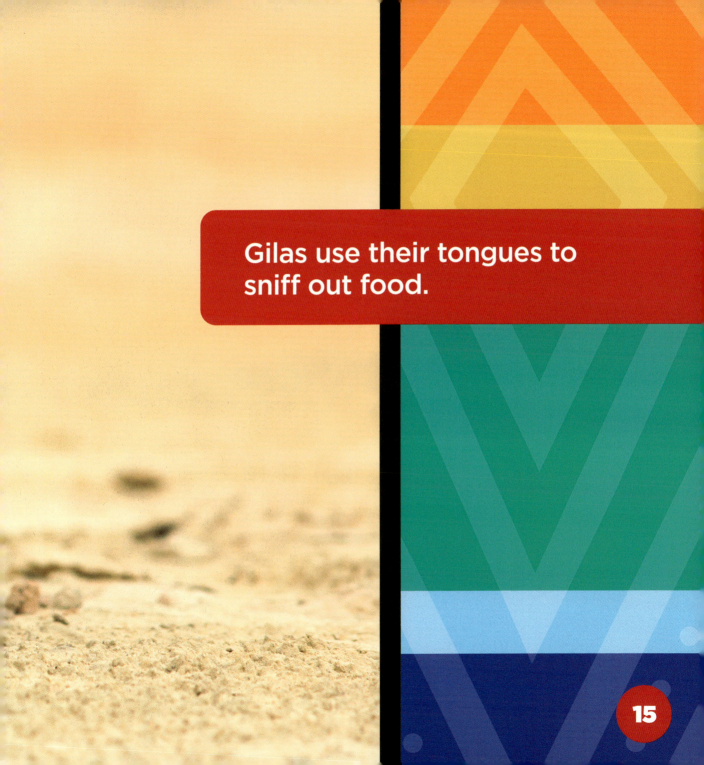

Gilas use their tongues to sniff out food.

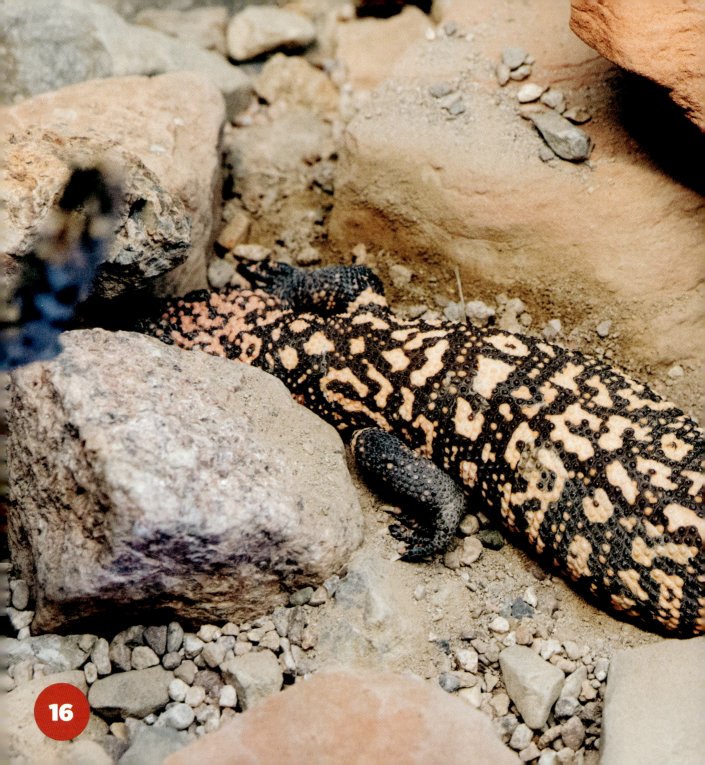

Female Gilas dig nests for their eggs. They lay up to 12 eggs at a time. Baby Gila are tiny at birth.

Gila monsters move slowly. They look like snakes with short legs.

18

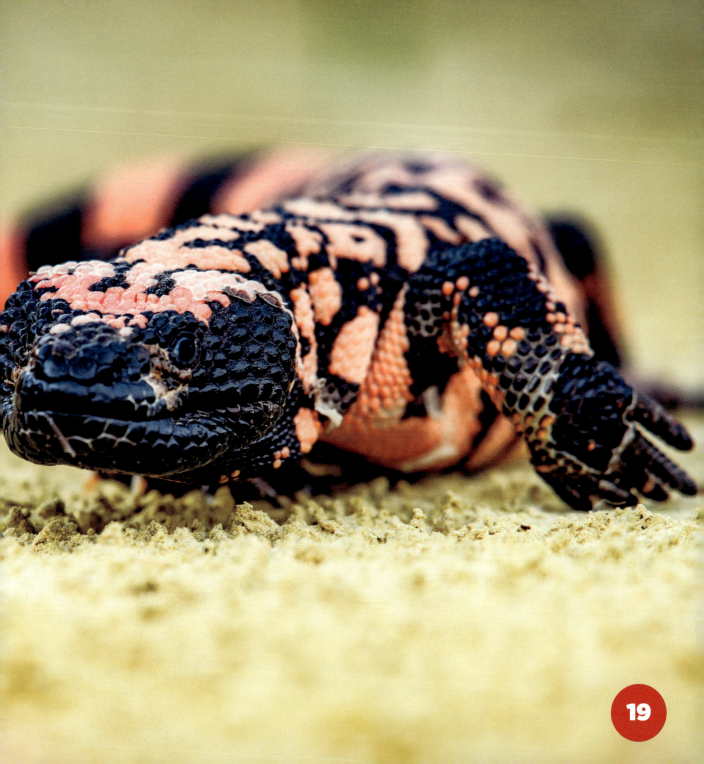

Gilas face dangers in the wild. Kids can help. Do not buy Gilas as pets.

# WHERE DO GILA MONSTERS LIVE?

The Gila monster lives primarily in Arizona and Mexico, the extreme southeastern corner of California, the southern tip of Nevada, and the southwestern corners of Utah and New Mexico.

22

## INTERESTING FACTS

- The Gila (say HEE-luh) is the largest lizard **native** to the United States.
- Gila monsters are good climbers. They will climb up a cactus to raid bird nests.
- The Gila monster hisses to scare enemies.
- They live about 20 years in the wild.
- One bite of a Gila monster will cause pain, swelling, and shock in humans.
- Gila monsters must drink lots of water in their dry, desert living places.
- Gila monsters walk high on their short legs, with the tail clear off the ground and swinging from side to side for balance.

## PARTS OF A GILA MONSTER

### Eyes
Gilas have black beady eyes that blend in with black scales in coloring.

### Skin
Gilas have scales over their bones that come in the shape of beads. The beads are arranged in colorful patterns on the head, tail, and skin.

### Tail
The Gila tail is 20 percent of its body length.

### Teeth
Gilas have big grooved teeth in their bottom jaws.

### Feet
Gilas have four feet with sharp claws, and there are five claws per foot.

# GLOSSARY

**burrow**
Den or hole in ground dug by animals

**forked**
Divided into two parts at one end; shaped like the letter Y

**native**
An animal that has lived in a place from the earliest times

**poisonous**
Containing a substance that can harm or kill a person or animal

**scales**
Small beadlike plates that cover all the Gila but its belly

# FURTHER READING

Glaser, John. *Gila Monsters*. Mankato, MN: Capstone Press, 2006.

Mattern, Joanne. *Gila Monsters*. Mankato, MN: Capstone Press, 2010.

# ON THE INTERNET

**Reptile Discovery Center, Smithsonian's National Zoo and Conservation Biology Institute**
https://nationalzoo.si.edu/animals/gila-monster

**Saint Louis Zoo. Saint Louis, Missouri**
https://www.stlzoo.org/animals/abouttheanimals/reptiles/lizards/bandedgilamonster

**Gila Monster; Animals, National Geographic**
https://www.nationalgeographic.com/animals/reptiles/g/gila-monster/

# INDEX

| | |
|---|---|
| Baby Gila | 17 |
| Deserts | 4, 23 |
| Frogs | 12 |
| Lizards | 4, 23 |
| Rodents | 12 |
| Scales | 9, 23 |
| Snakes | 18 |
| Worms | 12 |